The Story of Flight
MILITARY AIRCRAFT
of WWII

Crabtree Publishing Company
www.crabtreebooks.com

PMB 16A, 350 Fifth Avenue
Suite 3308
New York, NY 10118

612 Welland Avenue
St. Catharines, Ontario
L2M 5V6

Published in 2003 by
Crabtree Publishing Company

Coordinating editor: Ellen Rodger
Project editors: Sean Charlebois, Carrie Gleason
Production coordinator: Rose Gowsell

Created and Produced by
David West 👫 Children's Books

Project Development, Design, and Concept
David West Children's Books:
Designer: Rob Shone
Editor: James Pickering
Illustrators: Neil Reed (Allied Artists), James Field &
Ross Watton (SGA), Gary Slater & Steve Weston
(Specs Art), Alex Pang
Picture Research: Carlotta Cooper

Photo Credits:
Abbreviations: t-top, m-middle, b-bottom, r-right,
l-left, c-center.

Front cover tml & pages 26tl (P16370), 4tr (DB52
Siks), 5tr (FA10179), 6tl (PC 74/41/480) & br (PC
71/19/835), 8ml (PC 75/2/5360), 11mr (5993-13),
14tl (RAE Album), 16tl (P577), 17tm (PC
76/23/34), 18tl (PC 71/19/798) & bl (PC 95/21),
22tl (P7681), 24ml (5980-10), 27br (PC
75/2/5288), 29ml (PC 96/67) - Royal Air Force
Museum. 11tr - Novosti (London). 12tl, 13tr, 15tr,
29tr - Rex Features Ltd. 20tl & mr, 22ml - The Flight
Collection. 25tr - Hulton Getty Picture Collection.

06 05 04 03
10 9 8 7 6 5 4 3 2 1

Cataloging in Publication Data
Hansen, Ole Steen.
   Military aircraft of WWII / written by Ole Steen Hansen.
      p. cm. -- (The story of flight)
Includes index.
ISBN 0-7787-1203-6 (RLB) -- ISBN 0-7787-1219-2 (PB)
   1. Airplanes, Military--History--20th century--Juvenile literature.
   2. World War, 1939-1945--Aerial operations--Juvenile literature.
[1. Airplanes, Military 2. World War, 1939-1945--Aerial operations.]
I. Title.
   UG1240.H35697 2003
   940.54'4--dc21
                              2002156483
                              LC

The Story of Flight

MILITARY AIRCRAFT of WWII

Ole Steen Hansen

Crabtree Publishing Company
www.crabtreebooks.com

CONTENTS

SPANISH CIVIL WAR
Italy and Germany tested their new aircraft and weapons while fighting in the Spanish Civil War (1936–39). The bombing of Guernica, Spain, destroyed many homes. During World War II, the people of Europe faced the same kinds of attacks.

INTRODUCTION

World War II (1939–45) was the most destructive conflict in human history. Aircraft took part in every major battle. During the first years of the war, aircraft led the way for the advancing German tanks. Later, British, American, and Soviet airpower played a crucial role in defeating Germany and the Axis powers. Never before or since has the world seen aerial battles on such an enormous scale.

PROPAGANDA POSTER
British posters celebrated Germany's losses in the Battle of Britain and gave thanks to Britain's own fighter pilots.

STUKA
German Stuka dive-bombers spread terror in the early years of World War II. Here they are attacking British troops being evacuated from Dunkirk, France.

BATTLE OF BRITAIN

By the summer of 1940, the German army occupied Poland, France, and several other European countries. The British army, which included forces from Commonwealth nations such as Canada and Australia, had lost most of its equipment in Dunkirk, France, but still continued to fight to prevent Germany from invading Britain.

To invade Britain, the German army planned to use their air power to destroy the Royal Navy and other British defenses. Britain's Royal Air Force (RAF) needed to be eliminated so that German aviators would be free from attack. Destroying the British fighter planes proved to be easier said than done. The long weeks of fierce aerial combat over southern England became known as the Battle of Britain. At first, the German attacks concentrated on the RAF fighter airfields. Later, they attacked London. They hoped to destroy the city and the **morale** of the British people.

REGINALD MITCHELL

Aircraft designer Reginald Mitchell was seriously ill with cancer when he designed the Spitfire. He believed Britain would soon need a fighter plane to defend the country.

In The Right Place At The Right Time

Germany had more fighter planes than Britain during the Battle of Britain. Thanks to radar, a device that uses reflected radio waves to locate planes, British fighter planes were usually in the right place at the right time. Reports from radar stations were sent to rooms (right) where attacking **formations** were tracked. British fighters were then directed toward the enemy.

DOGFIGHT
British Spitfires and German Messerschmitt 109s circled around each other over southern England in what came to be called "dogfights."

Instead, the attacks on London allowed the RAF to recover and fight the **Luftwaffe** in the air. In the end, German losses mounted and the attacks ended. It was the first time the Germans were stopped. It was an important turning point in the war for the **Allies**. In the following years, Britain became the base where the Allies built up forces to **liberate** Europe.

SPITFIRE

The Spitfire first flew in 1936 and was a very advanced aircraft for its time. Designed in an age when RAF fighters were fabric-covered two gun **biplanes**, the Spitfire had an all-metal construction and was armed with eight machine-guns. It was fast, highly maneuverable, had a retractable **undercarriage**, and was a pilot's dream to fly. It also had great potential for further development.

Reginald Mitchell only saw the very first Spitfire fly before he died in 1937. About 21,500 Spitfires in more than 20 different versions, including "Seafires" for naval use, were built up to 1949.

WAR IN THE DESERT

In Africa, German and Italian forces tried to push British troops back over the sandy and rocky wastes of the northern Sahara. It was a war fought over long open distances. Fuel, supplies, troops, and ammunition were brought to the battlefront. Aircraft were used to prevent German supplies from making it to the front.

HANS-JOACHIM MARSEILLE

Hans-Joachim Marseille, a 22-year-old German ace born in Berlin, was a deadly aim, who once shot down 17 British aircraft in a single day. Despite aces such as Marseille, eventually the masses of Allied aircraft proved impossible for the Germans to stop.

Supply And Demand

The Germans tried in vain to reinforce the Africa Korps by flying in fuel and ammunition. They used Junkers 52 transport aircraft and the giant six-engined Messerschmitt Me 323 seen here. The heavy losses hit the Germans very hard, because many of the transport pilots were instructors, transferred from flying schools. Their deaths made it difficult for the Germans to train new pilots.

The battles raged from late 1940 to May 1943 when the German Africa Korps finally surrendered in Tunisia. The Germans fought under the leadership of General Erwin Rommel, who was often called "the desert fox." In the end, the Germans lost to the Allied forces. The battle of El Alamein in Egypt in 1942 was the turning point. Shortly after, fresh U.S. and British forces landed in French North Africa. Aircraft played an important part in defeating the Germans. The Allied aircraft attacked German positions and made it impossible for the Germans to bring in supplies.

DESERT HURRICANE

In the Battle of Britain, pilots flew Hurricane fighters, but the planes were becoming obsolete. In the desert, they were used as ground attack aircraft. A sand-filter was attached to the plane to protect the engine from dust, and it was armed with guns that could shoot at tanks. Many German vehicles and tanks were destroyed by Hurricanes. Pilots had to be careful firing the heavy guns when they were attacking from low-level, because the aircraft often fell nose-first into the sand from the weight of the guns.

Countless German trucks were shot to pieces in the desert, and large numbers of ships were sunk on their way from Italy. The German Chancellor Adolf Hitler made the mistake of committing the air force to supply the remnants of the Africa Korps in Tunisia. In the last six months of the desert war, Germany lost 2,400 aircraft.

SHARK MOUTH P-40

American-built Curtiss P-40 fighters were used by Britain's Royal Air Force in the desert. An American volunteer group, called "The Flying Tigers," flew P-40s against the Japanese in the Pacific.

NORTH AFRICA

WINTER ON THE EASTERN FRONT
Lilya Litvyak flew combat missions during the Battle of Stalingrad in the winter of 1943. She mostly flew the Yak-1 and was injured three times.

PO-2
The all-female 588th Night Bomber Regiment flew two-seater PO-2s. These small biplanes were built more for training than bombing, but they were very effective for carrying out raids behind enemy lines.

WOMEN AT WAR

The Soviet Union fought desperately to stop the German advance to the east in 1941. Millions of Soviet soldiers were killed or captured. It took an all-out effort from every Soviet to produce weapons for defense and to use them. The Soviet Union was the only fighting power where women performed combat duties.

LILYA LITVYAK

Lilya Litvyak was the highest scoring Soviet female fighter pilot. She flew 168 missions and shot down 12 German planes. She was only 21 when she was killed in combat with German fighters in 1943.

Most Soviet soldiers during World War II were men. There were fewer than 1,000 Soviet airwomen, and they had to prove themselves. Many men believed that women could not handle the terrors and techniques of combat. Soviet women flew bombers, fighters, and **reconnaissance** aircraft. Sometimes they flew in mixed units together with men, while other units were made up entirely of female air and ground crews. They flew thousands of **sorties** attacking German positions, camps, and depots. They flew in the big battle of Stalingrad, in many smaller ones across the vast rolling steppes, and in the final battle for Berlin. Two female bomber pilots even flew 18 raids in a single night!

Women In The Air Force

Women served in many non-combat functions. In the United States, some members of the Women's Army Auxillary Corps (WAAC) served at Aircraft Warning Service Stations. In Britain, members of the WAAF (Women Auxillary Air Force) worked in air traffic control, planning, intelligence, and **meteorology**. Women in both Britain and the United States flew new aircraft from the factories to Air Force bases.

After a long day's fighting, the German soldiers badly needed rest, but the PO-2s prevented them from getting any. The Germans feared the female bomber crews and called them "Night Witches."

WAR IN THE PACIFIC

ZERO

The Japanese Zero was an excellent fighter, with a very long range. It took the Allied powers completely by surprise at the beginning of the war in Asia.

In the Pacific, Japan tried to expand its territory. Japanese forces fought numerous battles with American troops on many Pacific islands. It quickly became clear that battleships with heavy guns were no match for light bombers flying from aircraft carriers. The aircraft carrier became the most powerful weapon at sea.

The surprise attack on Pearl Harbor was not a great success for the Japanese. American aircraft carriers were at sea, so they survived the attack. The carriers helped to turn the tide in the Pacific war in just six months. In May 1942, the Japanese expansion was stopped in the Coral Sea at the first battle in history fought exclusively with aircraft flying from carriers. In June 1942, the Japanese suffered a serious defeat in the Battle of Midway because of aircraft attacks. The Japanese Navy never recovered from the loss of its aircraft carriers. On the other hand, the United States, with its massive industrial strength, soon had 131 carriers on order or under construction in the shipyards.

Day Of Infamy

The United States was drawn into World War II on December 7, 1941 when Pearl Harbor, Hawaii, was attacked by Japanese aircraft flying from six aircraft carriers. The surprise attack killed 2,400 Americans and 18 ships were hit. The President called it a day that would live in infamy.

PACIFIC OCEAN

DAUNTLESS DIVE-BOMBER

The Battle of Midway was won by U.S. Navy Dauntless dive-bombers which hit the enemy carriers in a matter of minutes. Most bombs missed their targets, but the few hits created large unstoppable fires in the Japanese carriers.

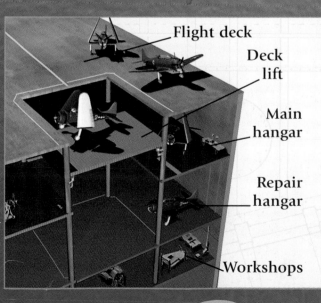

Flight deck

Deck lift

Main hangar

Repair hangar

Workshops

FLOATING AIRFIELDS

Aircraft carriers were like floating airfields. Below the flight deck were hangars for the aircraft, repair facilities, sleeping quarters for the crew, and storage rooms for fuel and weapons. Huge carriers with aircraft could hit targets harder and further away than any other ships. Carriers were also very vulnerable and had to be protected by smaller ships and their own fighter planes.

RECONNAISSANCE

The smallest military aircraft of World War II were also some of the most feared by soldiers on the ground. Small artillery spotter planes would pinpoint targets and direct the guns. A Piper Cub or an Auster might be unarmed, but over the radio the pilot could order more than 70 guns to fire.

The sight of an artillery spotter plane could silence the enemy for fear of being spotted. These small planes were also used for many other jobs near the front. They flew VIPs, casualties, and, sometimes, supplies to forward units.

EYE IN THE SKY
This camera is mounted in the fuselage of a Spitfire. Unarmed photo reconnaissance Spitfires flew high and fast, deep inside enemy territory to photograph targets.

FIESLER FI 156 STORCH
This German multi-role observation plane could take off and land in very short distances.

Length: 32 ft 6 in (9.9 m)
Wingspan: 46 ft 9 in (14.3 m)
Speed: 109 mph (175 km/h)

FLYING FRAMES
The fuselages of the Piper Cub and Auster were built from welded steel tubes and covered in fabric. This offered no protection from ground fire, but neither did the thin metal skins of the heavier fighters and bombers. In fact, the steel tube fuselage was very strong in a crash, which happened when pilots flew low between trees and haystacks – or sometimes accidentally into them!

Officers were taken up to get a view of the ground over which they would soon have to fight. A few Piper Cubs were armed with **bazookas** and used for attacking tanks, but that was never their main purpose.

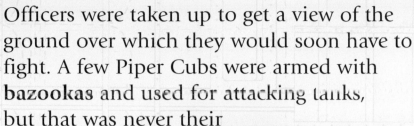

PIPER CUB
This pre-war American training aircraft was useful for artillery spotting.

Length: 22 ft 5 in (6.9 m)
Wingspan: 35 ft 3 in (10.8 m)
Speed: 85 mph (136 km/h)

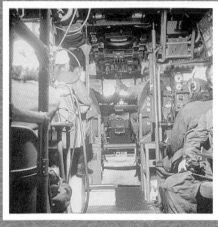

Ocean Patrol
Crew members worked inside the huge flying boats which flew long patrols over the sea. During World War II, German U-boat submarines sailed on the surface to catch up with other ships. A flying boat could patrol vast areas of sea and force a U-boat to dive. This prevented the U-boat from attacking, even if the flying boat did not hit it. The picture above shows the interior of a Japanese Kawanishi flying boat in 1945.

The artillery spotters flew from unprepared grassy fields very close to the **front line**. The pilots and ground crew slept in tents and moved forward with the armies.

AUSTER MK III
The British Army used Austers for artillery observation. They were developed in many different versions.

Length: 22 ft 11 in (7 m)
Wingspan: 36 ft 2 in (11.1 m)
Speed: 130 mph (208 km/h)

NIGHT BOMBERS

From the beginning of the war, the Royal Air Force Bomber Command fought against Germany. Eventually, pilots from all over the world flew with the British bombers. Belgians, Canadians, Danes, Poles, Australians, New Zealanders, South Africans, Norwegians, and pilots from many other nations flew to help liberate Europe. Every RAF bomber pilot was a volunteer.

BOMBER HARRIS

Sir Arthur Harris, known as "Bomber Harris," commanded RAF Bomber Command from February 1942. He was ordered to let his bombers concentrate on bombing the houses of the German people.

Some leading officers in the RAF hoped Germany would give up if its cities were bombed heavily enough. During the early war years, military targets, oil refineries, and railways were attacked. In 1941, Bomber Command realized that very few of its bombs hit anywhere near their targets. The strategy was then changed from pinpoint attacks to general area bombing of German cities. The houses of the German workers and other civilians were made targets and bombed.

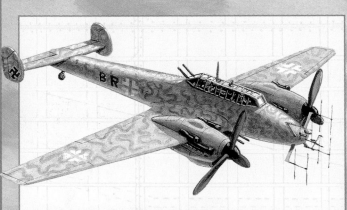

ELECTRONIC WARFARE

The British bombers flew at night to hide from the German defenses. This made it very difficult for them to find their targets. As the years went by, better radar and other electronic devices made it possible to pinpoint targets at night. It also made it possible for the German night fighters to find the bombers. The night battles became deadly electronic games of hide-and-seek. German night fighters such as this Me 110 inflicted heavy losses on the British bombers.

Germany had to be defeated, and at the start of the war RAF Bomber Command was the only force able to hit Germany directly. The bombings did not cause Hitler to give up, but the massive damage to their cities made the German war plans harder to carry out.

Andrew Charles Mynarski VC
Canadian aviator Andrew Charles Mynarski was mid-upper **gunner** on a Lancaster bomber that was hit, trapping the rear gunner in his seat. Mynarski could have jumped, but he went back through the flames to help. Beating and hammering away, Mynarski had to give up and finally jumped with his own clothes and parachute a mass of flames. Miraculously, the rear gunner survived the crash. Mynarski landed in occupied France but died from severe burns. He was awarded the Victoria Cross after his death.

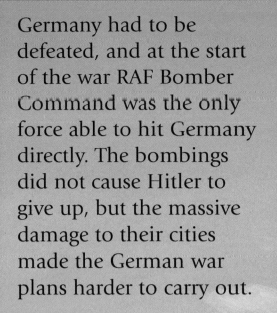

HOME WITH THE DAWN
Night bomber crews had only a 25 percent chance of surviving their flights unharmed. Watching the break of dawn on their return was a very emotional moment for the crews. It meant they had survived another raid.

PRECISION BOMBING

It was very difficult to hit precise targets during World War II. More often, whole parts of a town were bombed. Some specially trained squadrons were capable of hitting small targets with great accuracy. One such raid was the bombing of three buildings used by the German secret police, or Gestapo, in the city of Aarhus, Denmark in 1944.

The Gestapo headquarters in Aarhus was bombed because the Germans were close to destroying the **resistance movement** in Denmark. The British did not want to harm Danish citizens living nearby, so they only targeted these three buildings.

DAMBUSTERS

In May 1943, modified Lancasters, flown by crews trained especially for the mission, attacked and destroyed two German dams on the Ruhr River.

Barnes Wallis

Barnes Wallis was the engineer who designed airships and the Vickers Wellington bomber in the 1930s. During World War II he designed the "skipping bombs" that bounced across the water and smashed the German dams. This was an attempt to stop German war production by means other than burning down cities. After the war, he worked on supersonic swing-wing jets.

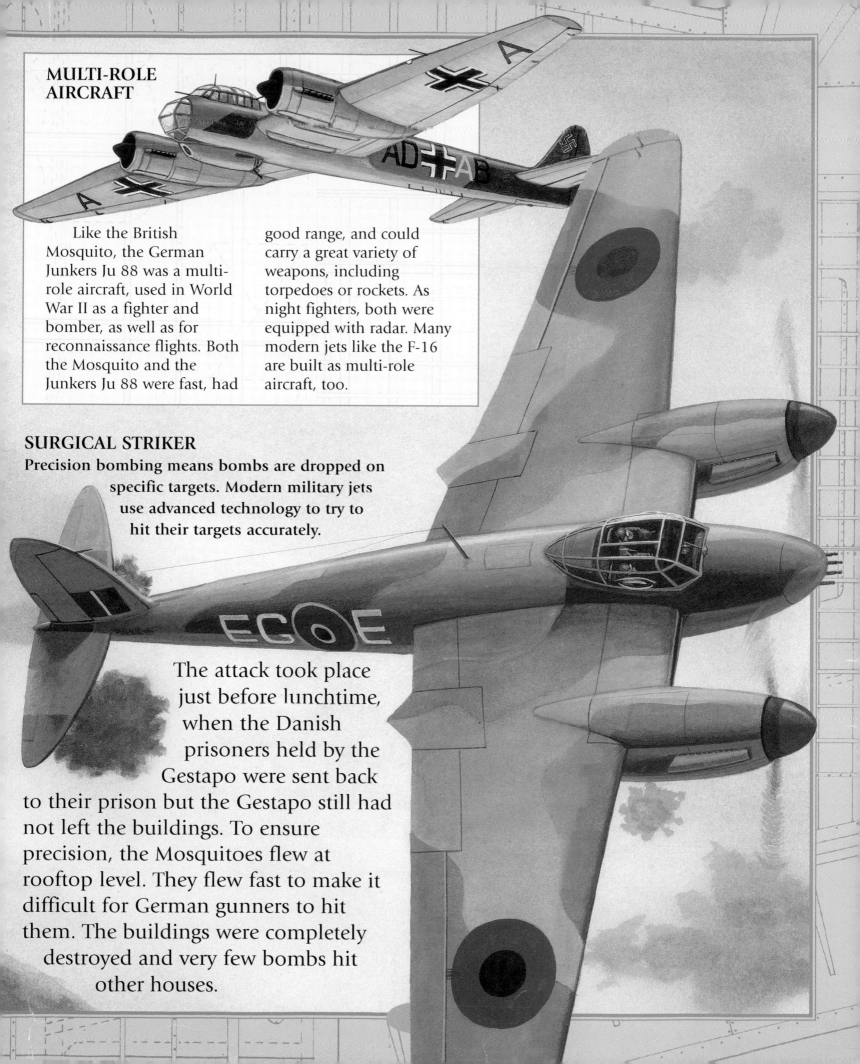

MULTI-ROLE AIRCRAFT

Like the British Mosquito, the German Junkers Ju 88 was a multi-role aircraft, used in World War II as a fighter and bomber, as well as for reconnaissance flights. Both the Mosquito and the Junkers Ju 88 were fast, had good range, and could carry a great variety of weapons, including torpedoes or rockets. As night fighters, both were equipped with radar. Many modern jets like the F-16 are built as multi-role aircraft, too.

SURGICAL STRIKER

Precision bombing means bombs are dropped on specific targets. Modern military jets use advanced technology to try to hit their targets accurately.

The attack took place just before lunchtime, when the Danish prisoners held by the Gestapo were sent back to their prison but the Gestapo still had not left the buildings. To ensure precision, the Mosquitoes flew at rooftop level. They flew fast to make it difficult for German gunners to hit them. The buildings were completely destroyed and very few bombs hit other houses.

TRANSPORTERS

The Wright Flyer of 1903 - the very first powered aircraft to fly - was barely able to lift itself and its pilot. Just 40 years later, during World War II, transport aircraft carried heavy loads to help win the war.

DAKOTA DROPS

The American Douglas C-47, called Dakota in the RAF, was used to drop paratroopers, tow gliders, fly supplies to forward units in combat zones, and evacuate the wounded. The C-47 was based on the famous DC-3 passenger aircraft that was developed in 1935.

Transport aircraft were used to drop **paratroopers** behind enemy lines. They also brought supplies to troops surrounded by the enemy. Many wounded soldiers were flown from the front line to better equipped hospitals away from the fighting. Aircraft also made it possible to supply resistance movements in occupied Europe. They flew secret agents, weapons, explosives, and radio equipment to these armies. Details of where and when the drops would take place were given in code via radio programs. The airplane and radio made it possible for resistance movements to co-ordinate their operations with the war efforts of the free world.

Tante Ju
The most widely used German transporter was the rugged and dependable Junkers Ju 52, popularly known as "Tante Ju," "Auntie Ju," or "Iron Annie." It was a pre-war airliner, like the American DC-3 Dakota, that was put into use as a military transport plane. Tante Jus were built throughout the war.

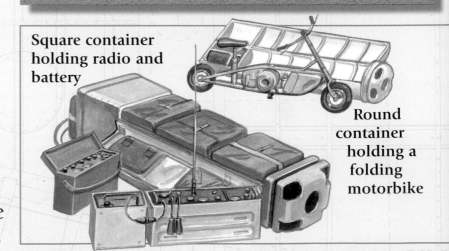

Square container holding radio and battery

Round container holding a folding motorbike

LYSANDER PICK-UP

Royal Air Force Lysander aircraft were fitted with long range fuel tanks. They flew agents in and out of occupied France from the secret Tempsford air base north of London. The Lysanders landed by moonlight on grass fields, quickly exchanged their passengers, and took off again as soon as possible.

EQUIPMENT

Weapons, radios, explosives, and other kinds of equipment were packed in containers and dropped from aircraft to supply troops or resistance movements. These drops could be very risky since they had to be made from low level and near enemy troops. Often, the supplies were never found.

WAR OVER GERMANY

DEFENDERS OF THE REICH
The Germans had great difficulty replacing the losses they suffered in combat with American fighters. In the summer of 1944, the average German fighter pilot had less than 30 hours combat experience.

The Mustang Prototype
North American P-51 Mustangs had American-built airframes and British-made Rolls-Royce Merlin engines. The Mustang was designed by a self-taught German immigrant who had worked for the German company Messerschmitt in the 1930s. Mustangs defeated the Luftwaffe fighters and made the American bombings of Germany possible. The Mustang first flew in 1940 and continued to be made for nine years.

The United States started bombing Germany in 1943. They did so in daylight, believing that big formations of bombers, armed with plenty of machine-guns, would be able to shoot their way through the fighter defenses.

This proved to be a costly mistake, because instead of trying to hide under cover of darkness, the Americans built thousands of long range P-51 Mustang fighters to protect the day bombers over Germany. In 1944, this resulted in the largest air battles ever fought. Hundreds of B-17s, or "Flying Fortresses" knocked out the German oil industry.

EUROPE

German fighters tried desperately to prevent this, but suffered terrible losses in combat with the Mustangs. The result of these battles was a serious German shortage of oil and trained fighter pilots. This helped the Allies win the war.

B-29 SUPERFORTRESS
The American B-29 Superfortress was the largest, fastest, and most advanced bomber of World War II. It was only used in the Pacific where its long range was necessary. In Europe, earlier versions of these bombers tried to hit oil refineries and other military targets. Over Japan, B-29s dropped **incendiaries** to burn down whole cities, much like the British bombers did over Germany.

FLYING IN FORMATION
Even though they flew in tight formations and had machine-guns, the American B-17 Flying Fortresses could not protect themselves.

23

NOW IT'S OUR TURN!
101st

22

Hawker Typhoon

Armed with rockets, Hawker Typhoon fighter bombers attacked German trucks and tanks after D-Day. The Germans were fighting almost as if they were isolated on an island. The fighter bombers made it extremely difficult for them to bring supplies and fresh troops forward to the Normandy battlefield.

D-DAY

On D-Day, June 6, 1944, Allied forces landed on the beaches of Normandy, France. Aircraft flew a total of 14,000 operations to support the Normandy landings. It was the greatest operation combining air, sea, and land forces ever launched.

U.S. and British air forces destroyed many bridges and railways all over France in the months leading up to D-Day. The night before D-Day, when the assault platoons were waiting in their landing craft by the shore, the air forces flew in airborne troops to secure bridges and confuse the German army. The morning bombardment of the German positions on the beaches was only a limited success. The heavy bombers flying from England were afraid of hitting the soldiers in the landing craft, and dropped their loads too far inland. During the day, thousands of Allied fighters flew so many patrols over Northern France that very few German aircraft got anywhere near the beaches.

GLIDERS

Some airborne troops landed by parachute while others were flown in assault gliders. Gliders were also used to fly in reinforcements late on D-Day afternoon.

NORMANDY

ON THE BEACHES

On the beaches of Normandy, the infantry waded ashore, and began fighting to liberate occupied Europe. Without the navy to get them there, and without the air force to provide support, the D-Day operation would not have been possible.

Main parachute

Life-jacket

Reserve parachute

Kit bag

British drop bag

Knife

PARATROOPS

Paratroopers were heavily loaded with equipment. They typically carried weapons such as rifles, pistols, and knives, as well as 160 rounds of ammunition, four grenades, an anti-tank mine, field rations for three days, first aid kit, and parts for mortars, machine-guns, or radios. One American paratrooper discovered that while his own body weight was 136 lb (62 kg), his parachute and equipment weighed a total of 176 lb (80 kg)!

THE FIRST JETS

During World War II, the first jets were used in combat. The jet engine was invented before the war, but air force generals in all countries were slow to see how it could be used for military purposes. By the war's end, Germany had produced more jets than any other nation.

FRANK WHITTLE
Royal Air Force officer Frank Whittle invented the jet engine in the 1930s but found little support for his project.

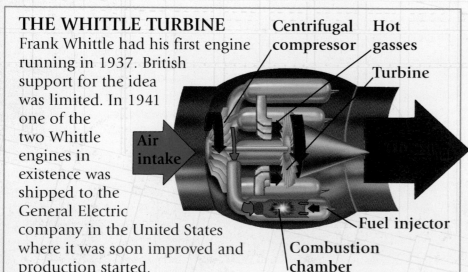

MESSERSCHMITT ME 262
Country: Germany
Description: Fighter bomber
Length: 34 ft 9 in (10.6 m)
Wingspan: 40 ft 11 in (12.5 m)
Speed: 540 mph (864 km/h)
First Flight: 18 July 1942

THE WHITTLE TURBINE
Frank Whittle had his first engine running in 1937. British support for the idea was limited. In 1941 one of the two Whittle engines in existence was shipped to the General Electric company in the United States where it was soon improved and production started.

Centrifugal compressor
Hot gasses
Turbine
Air intake
Fuel injector
Combustion chamber

As the war dragged on, Germany realized it could not build more aircraft than the Soviet Union, the United States, and Britain combined. Germany hoped to win the air war by building better aircraft, preferably jet powered ones. Some of the German attempts to build jets turned out to be disastrous, while others

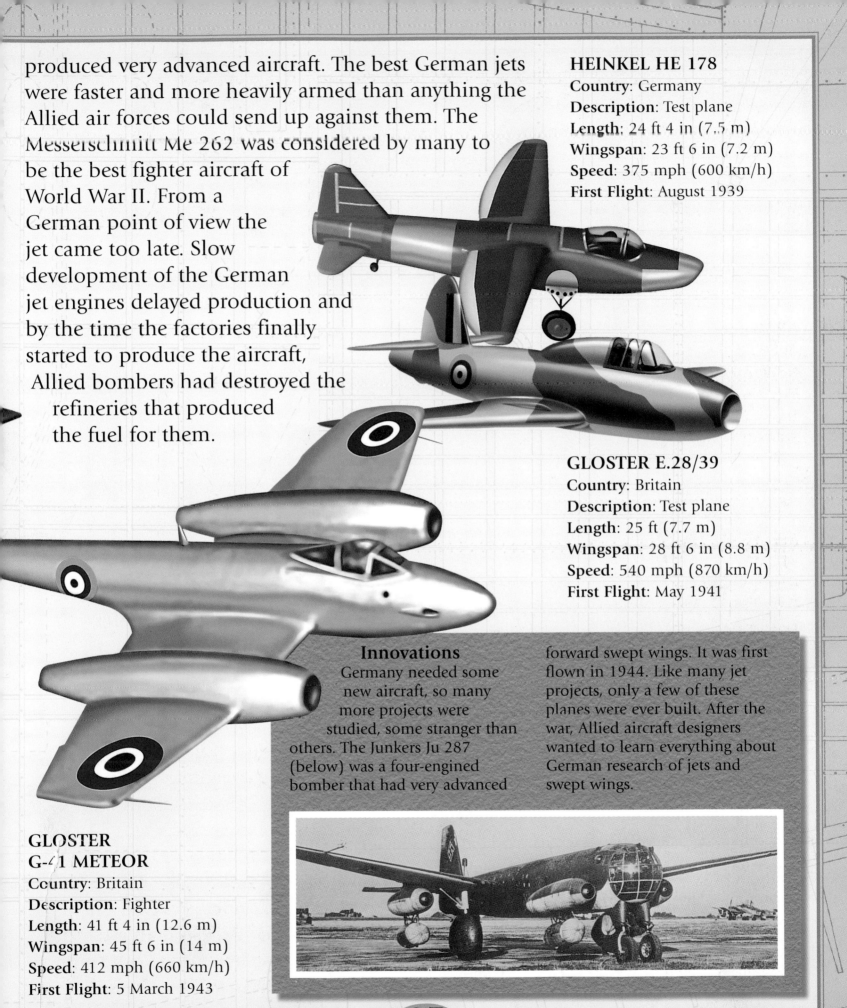

produced very advanced aircraft. The best German jets were faster and more heavily armed than anything the Allied air forces could send up against them. The Messerschmitt Me 262 was considered by many to be the best fighter aircraft of World War II. From a German point of view the jet came too late. Slow development of the German jet engines delayed production and by the time the factories finally started to produce the aircraft, Allied bombers had destroyed the refineries that produced the fuel for them.

HEINKEL HE 178
Country: Germany
Description: Test plane
Length: 24 ft 4 in (7.5 m)
Wingspan: 23 ft 6 in (7.2 m)
Speed: 375 mph (600 km/h)
First Flight: August 1939

GLOSTER E.28/39
Country: Britain
Description: Test plane
Length: 25 ft (7.7 m)
Wingspan: 28 ft 6 in (8.8 m)
Speed: 540 mph (870 km/h)
First Flight: May 1941

Innovations

Germany needed some new aircraft, so many more projects were studied, some stranger than others. The Junkers Ju 287 (below) was a four-engined bomber that had very advanced forward swept wings. It was first flown in 1944. Like many jet projects, only a few of these planes were ever built. After the war, Allied aircraft designers wanted to learn everything about German research of jets and swept wings.

**GLOSTER
G-41 METEOR**
Country: Britain
Description: Fighter
Length: 41 ft 4 in (12.6 m)
Wingspan: 45 ft 6 in (14 m)
Speed: 412 mph (660 km/h)
First Flight: 5 March 1943

LAST COMBATS

One Me 163 shot down a British bomber in April 1945, using a weapon that automatically fired rockets from the wing when a bomber passed overhead. It was another German weapon that made no difference to the outcome of the war.

ROCKET POWER

German designers did not limit their research to jets. They also tried to use rocket power. This resulted in the V2, the world's first ballistic **military rocket**. It also led to the Messerschmitt Me 163, the fastest combat aircraft of World War II.

GODDARD
American physicist Robert H. Goddard launched the world's first liquid fuel rocket in 1926. His work greatly inspired Wernher von Braun.

Dr Wernher Von Braun
As a young man, Wernher von Braun (center) was already dreaming passionately about building rockets. He became a leading director of the Nazi rocket program and designed the V2. After the war, he surrendered to the Americans who also found his talents useful. He helped them to send satellites into space and astronauts to the Moon.

The V2 flew at a speed of nearly 3,700 mph (6,000 km/h), but it could not hit its targets precisely. Between September 1944 and March 1945 a total of 1,054 V2 rockets hit England, but only 517 fell on London. The V2 was used as a terror weapon to spread random death and destruction, but it could not delay the Allied victory. The same can be said of the small Me 163 rocket-powered fighter.

This was first tested as a glider, without engines. When powered, it climbed and flew much faster than any other aircraft, but only had fuel for a few minutes. The Me 163 was very difficult to handle and many were lost in accidents. Some exploded when traces of the dangerous rocket fuel were left in the tanks on landing.

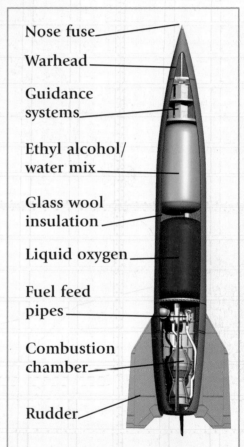

Nose fuse
Warhead
Guidance systems
Ethyl alcohol/water mix
Glass wool insulation
Liquid oxygen
Fuel feed pipes
Combustion chamber
Rudder

V2 ROCKET
The V2 engine burned its fuel in 65 seconds and flew up to a maximum altitude of 62 miles (100 km) from where it plunged down to its target. It was impossible to shoot down because it could not be heard approaching.

SPOTTERS' GUIDE

During World War II, fighters were small, fast, and easy to control. Bombers were big, heavy, and slow because they had to lift a heavy load. Bombers were armed with machine-guns to defend themselves, although this was a difficult task. The small Mosquito bomber was the shape of things to come. It carried the same bomb load as the B-17 but relied on speed to survive, which it did – very successfully.

**AVRO 683
LANCASTER**
Country: Britain
Description: Heavy bomber
Length: 69 ft 4 in (21.1 m)
Wingspan: 102 ft (31.1 m)
Speed: 287 mph (462 km/h)

YAKOVLEV YAK-1
Country: Soviet Union
Description: Fighter
Length: 27 ft 9in (8.5 m)
Wingspan: 32 ft 9 in (10 m)
Speed: 373 mph (600 km/h)

**CURTISS HAWK
P-40 KITTYHAWK**
Country: USA
Description: Single seat fighter
Length: 31 ft 2 in (9.5 m)
Wingspan: 37 ft 3 in (11.5 m)
Speed: 364 mph
(582 km/h)

SUPERMARINE SPITFIRE
Country: Britain
Description: Fighter
Length: 31 ft 3 in (9.5 m)
Wingspan: 36 ft 10 in (11.2 m)
Speed: 408 mph (657 km/h)

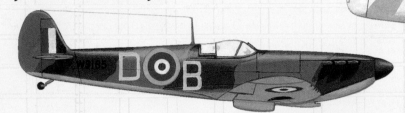

MESSERSCHMITT BF 109
Country: Germany
Description: Fighter
Length: 28 ft 4 in (8.6 m)
Wingspan: 32 ft 4 in (9.9 m)
Speed: 348 mph (560 km/h)

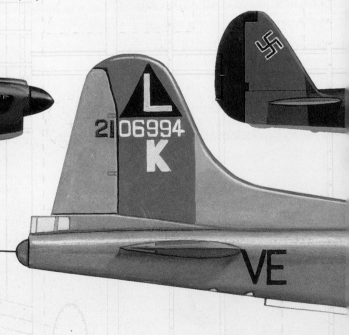

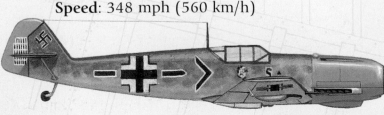

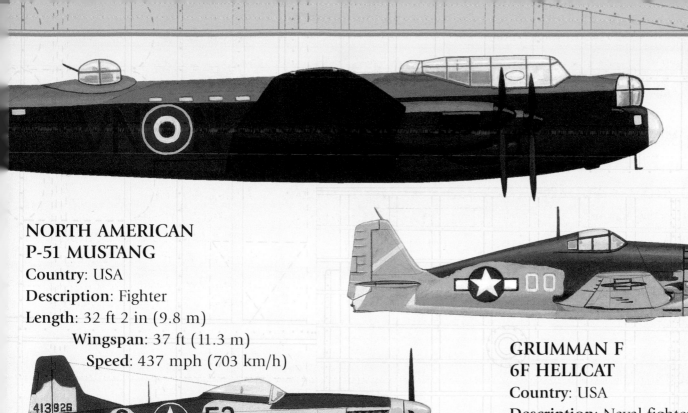

NORTH AMERICAN
P-51 MUSTANG
Country: USA
Description: Fighter
Length: 32 ft 2 in (9.8 m)
    Wingspan: 37 ft (11.3 m)
    Speed: 437 mph (703 km/h)

GRUMMAN F
6F HELLCAT
Country: USA
Description: Naval fighter bomber
Length: 33 ft 7 in (10.2 m)
Wingspan: 42 ft 10 in (13 m)
Speed: 376 mph (605 km/h)

JUNKERS JU 88
Country: Germany
Description: Dive bomber/night fighter
Length: 47 ft 2 in (14.4 m)
Wingspan: 65 ft 10 in (20.1 m)
Speed: 269 mph (433 km/h)

DE HAVILLAND
98 MOSQUITO
Country: Britain
Description: High-speed day bomber
Length: 40 ft 6 in (12.3 m)
Wingspan: 54 ft 2 in (16.5 m)
Speed: 410 mph (660 km/h)

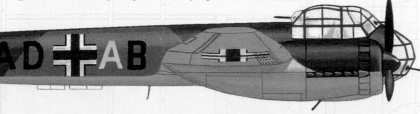

BOEING B-17 FLYING FORTRESS
Country: USA
    Description: High-altitude
    bomber
    Length: 74 ft 9 in (22.8 m)
    Wingspan: 103 ft 9 in
    (31.6 m)
    Speed: 287 mph (462 km/h)

INDEX

GLOSSARY

ALLIES The nations that fought together against the Axis powers in WWII, including Britain, France, the United States, and the Soviet Union.

AXIS POWERS The nations that fought in WWII against the Allies, including Germany, Italy, and Japan.

BALLISTIC Relating to the motion of projectiles, such as missiles.

BAZOOKA A weapon held on the shoulder that fires rockets.

BIPLANE An airplane with two sets of wings, one above the other.

DIVE-BOMBERS Aircraft that plunged downward to drop bombs.

FORMATION A particular arrangement of planes in flight.

FRONT LINE The forward position of troops.

FUSELAGE The body of an airplane to which the wings and tail are attached.

GLIDER An aircraft without an engine that glides on currents of air.

GUNNER A military person whose job it is to fire large guns.

INCENDIARY A kind of bomb that produces a hot fire when exploded.

LIBERATE To set free.

LUFTWAFFE The German air force during WWII.

METEOROLOGY The scientific study of the weather.

MORALE The state of mind of a person or group.

PARATROOPER A soldier trained to parachute from airplanes.

RANGE The distance an aircraft is capable of flying with the fuel it has.

RECONNAISSANCE The gathering of military information.

RESISTANCE MOVEMENT An underground or secret organization that works to oppose a government or military force.

SORTIE The flight of a combat aircraft on a mission.

UNDERCARRIAGE The supporting framework of a vehicle, such as an airplane.